Thinking Skills for Tests

Early Learning

WORKBOOK *

*For test administration instructions and answers,
please see Instruction/Answer Guide, 04502GBP, available separately.

Thinking Skills for Tests products available in print or eBook form.

Early Learning (PreK-2) • Upper Elementary (Grades 3-5)

Written by
Robin MacFarlane, Ph.D.

Graphic Design by
Scott Slyter

© 2011
THE CRITICAL THINKING CO.™
www.CriticalThinking.com
Phone: 800-458-4849 • Fax: 541-756-1758
1991 Sherman Ave., Suite 200 • North Bend • OR 97459
ISBN 978-1-60144-269-7

Reproduction of This Copyrighted Material

The intellectual material in this product is the copyrighted property of The Critical Thinking Co.™ The individual or entity who initially purchased this product from The Critical Thinking Co.™ or one of its authorized resellers is licensed to reproduce (print or duplicate on paper) each page of this product for use within one home or one classroom. Our copyright and this limited reproduction permission (user) agreement strictly prohibit the sale of any of the copyrighted material in this product. Any reproduction beyond these expressed limits is strictly prohibited without the written permission of The Critical Thinking Co.™ Please visit http://www.criticalthinking.com/copyright for more information. The Critical Thinking Co.™ retains full intellectual property rights on all its products (eBooks, books, and software).

Printed in China by Shanghai Chenxi Printing Co., Ltd. (Dec. 2018)

TABLE OF CONTENTS

© 2011 The Critical Thinking Co.™ • www.CriticalThinking.com • 800-458-4849

© 2011 The Critical Thinking Co.™ • www.CriticalThinking.com • 800-458-4849

© 2011 The Critical Thinking Co.™ • www.CriticalThinking.com • 800-458-4849

1.

2.

© 2011 The Critical Thinking Co.™ • www.CriticalThinking.com • 800-458-4849

3.

4.

5.

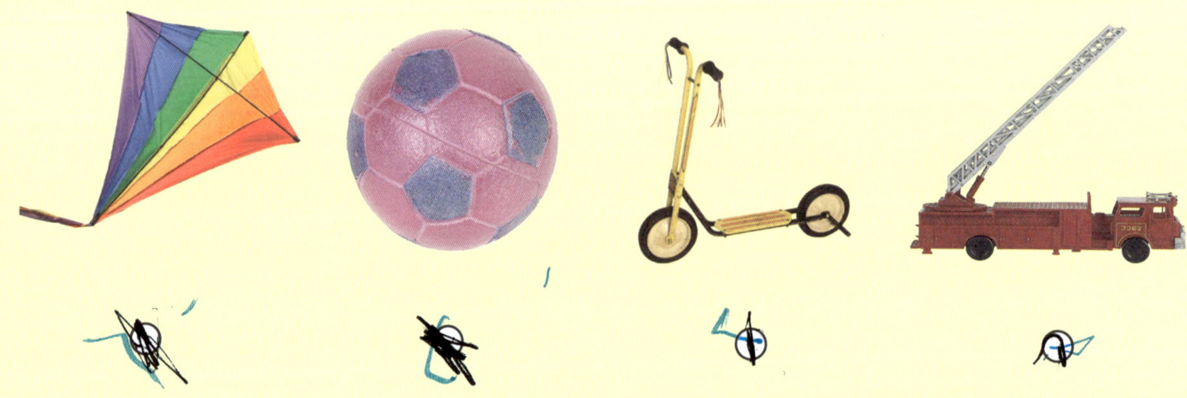

© 2011 The Critical Thinking Co.™ • www.CriticalThinking.com • 800-458-4849

6.

7.

8.

© 2011 The Critical Thinking Co.™ • www.CriticalThinking.com • 800-458-4849

9.

10.

11.

12.

© 2011 The Critical Thinking Co.™ • www.CriticalThinking.com • 800-458-4849

1.

2.

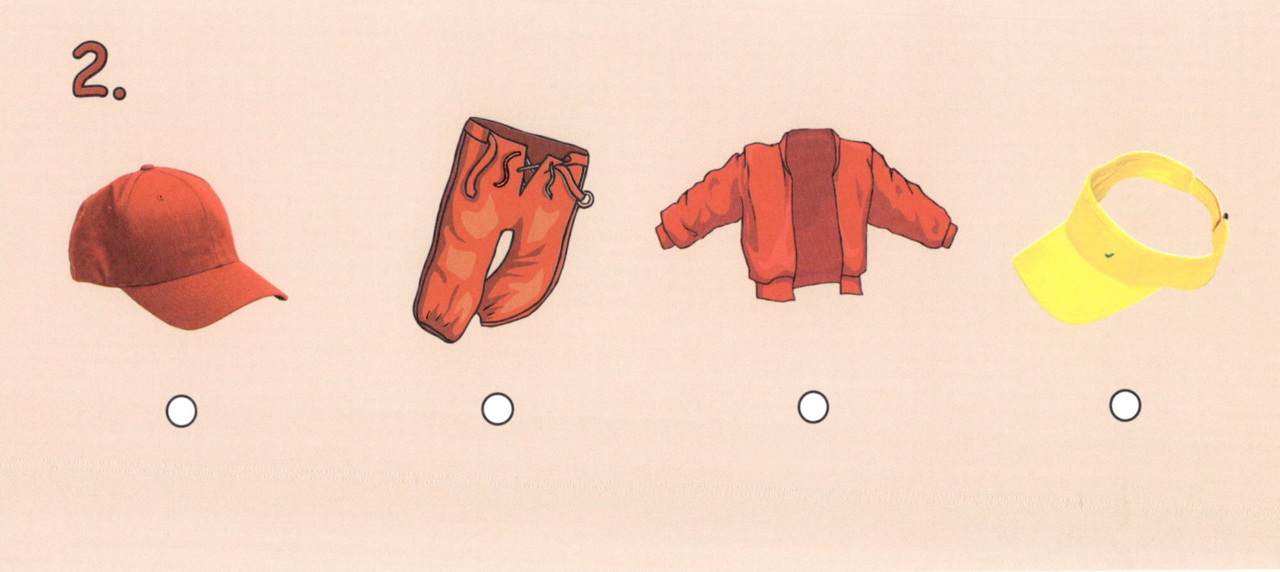

3.

4.

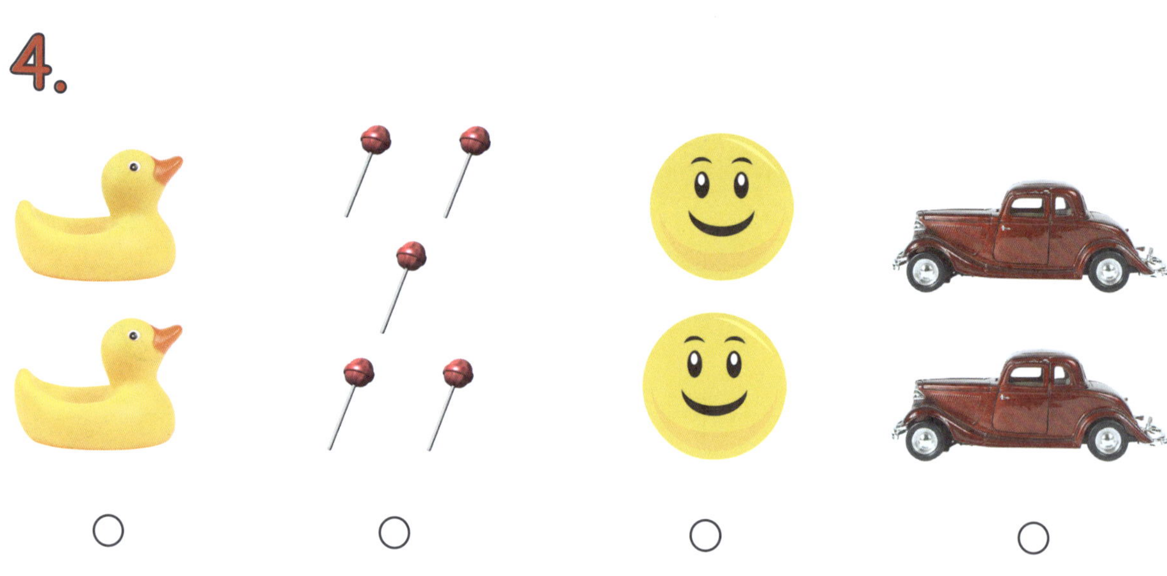

   ○   ○   ○   ○

5.

   ○   ○   ○   ○

© 2011 The Critical Thinking Co.™ • www.CriticalThinking.com • 800-458-4849

6.

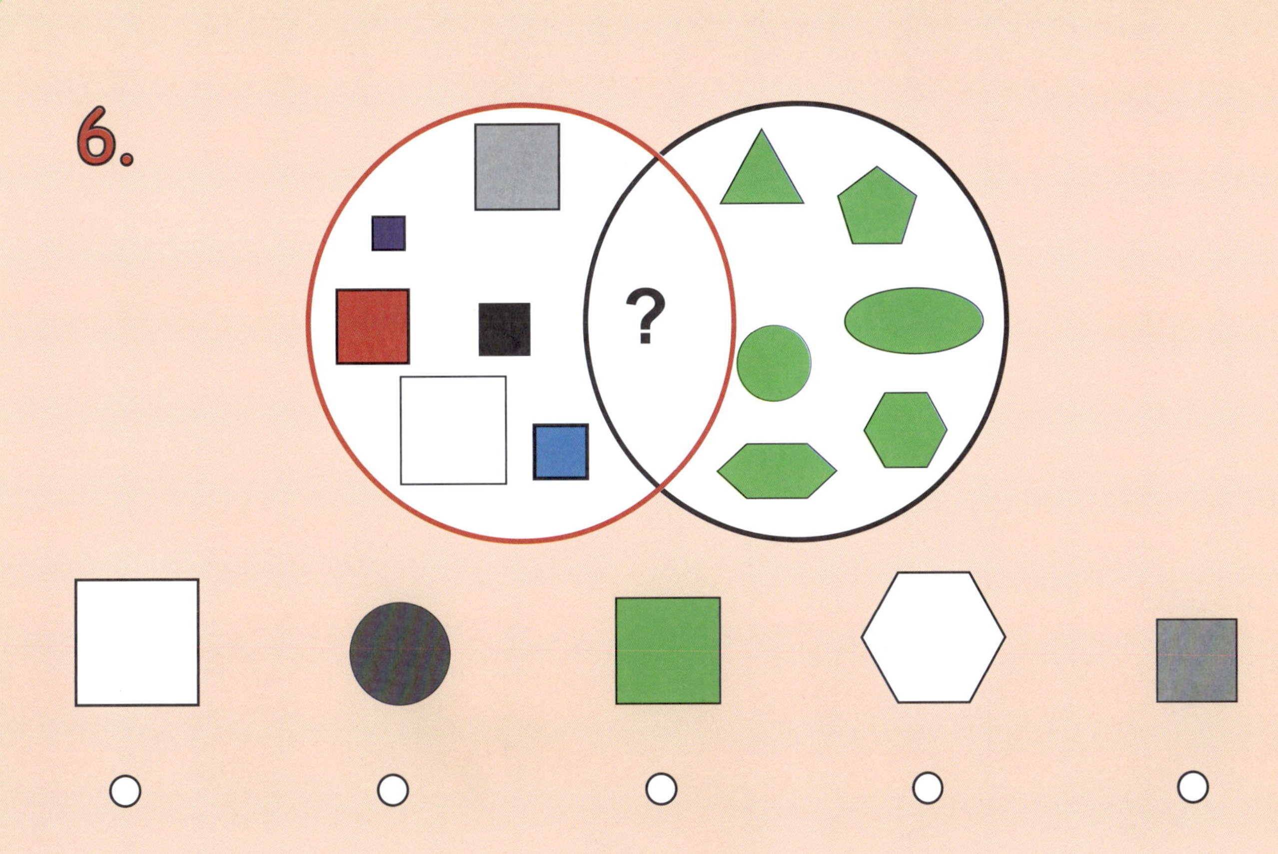

7.

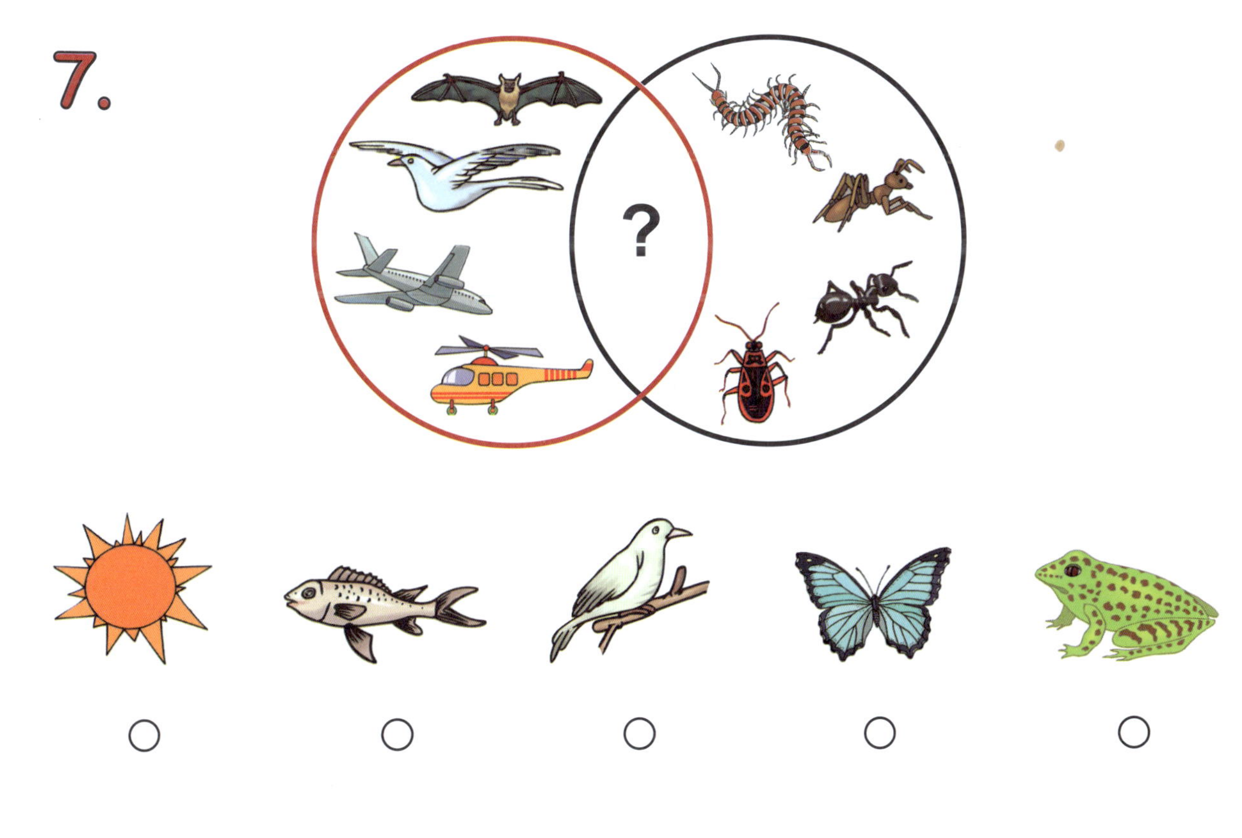

8.

9.

10.

© 2011 The Critical Thinking Co. ™ • www.CriticalThinking.com • 800-458-4849

11.

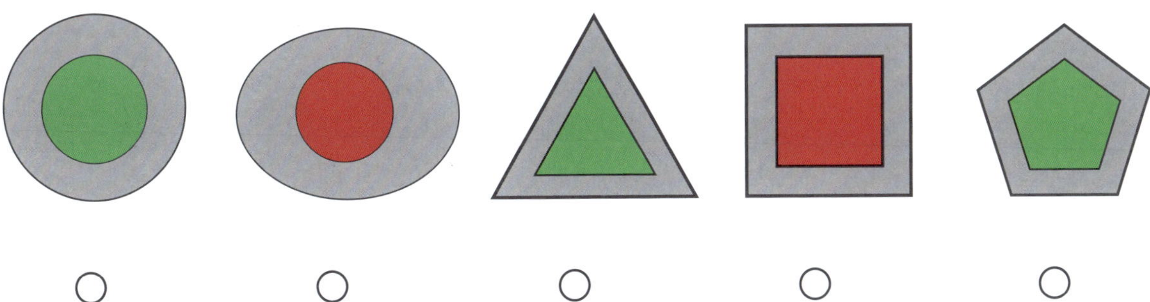

○   ○   ○   ○   ○

12.

○   ○   ○   ○   ○

1.

○   ○   ○   ○   ○

2.

○   ○   ○   ○

3.

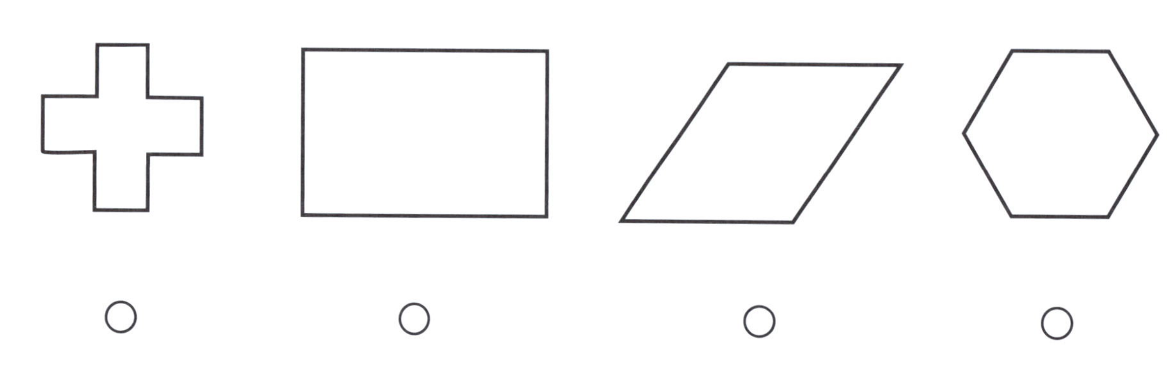

○   ○   ○   ○

© 2011 The Critical Thinking Co.™ • www.CriticalThinking.com • 800-458-4849

4.

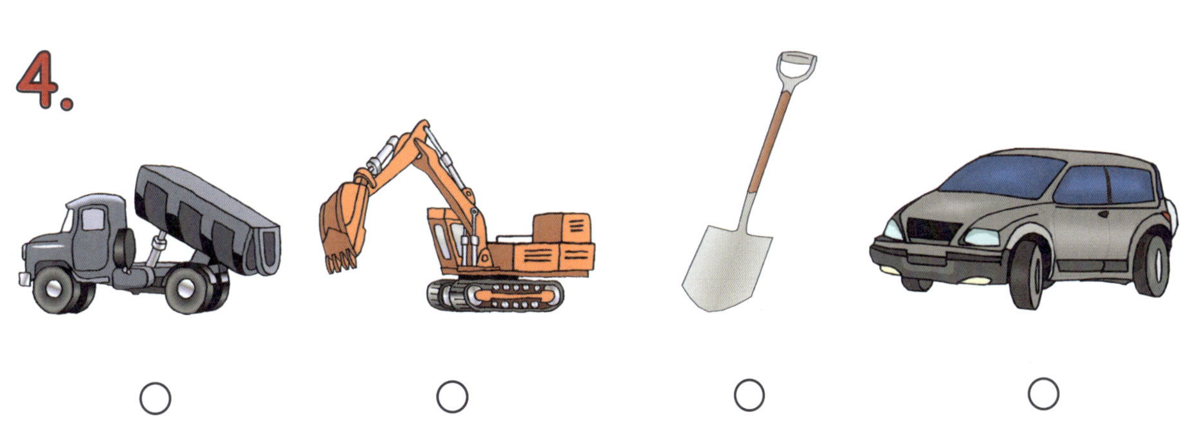

5.

6.

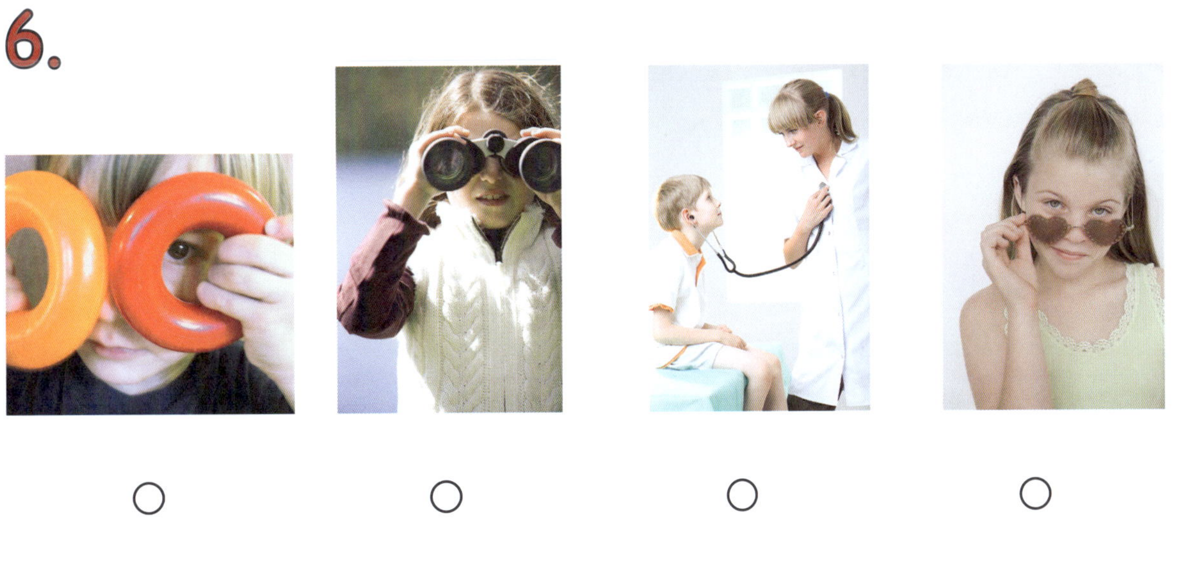

© 2011 The Critical Thinking Co.™ • www.CriticalThinking.com • 800-458-4849

7.

○　　　　○　　　　○　　　　○

8.

○　　　　○　　　　○　　　　○

© 2011 The Critical Thinking Co.™ • www.CriticalThinking.com • 800-458-4849

9.

○   ○   ○   ○

10.

○   ○   ○   ○

1.

2.

© 2011 The Critical Thinking Co.™ • www.CriticalThinking.com • 800-458-4849

3.

○

○

○

○

© 2011 The Critical Thinking Co.™ • www.CriticalThinking.com • 800-458-4849

4.

5.

6.

© 2011 The Critical Thinking Co.™ • www.CriticalThinking.com • 800-458-4849

7.

 ○

○ ○

8.

○ ○

○ ○

9.

© 2011 The Critical Thinking Co.™ • www.CriticalThinking.com • 800-458-4849

10.

◯   ◯   ◯   ◯

11.

◯   ◯   ◯   ◯

12.

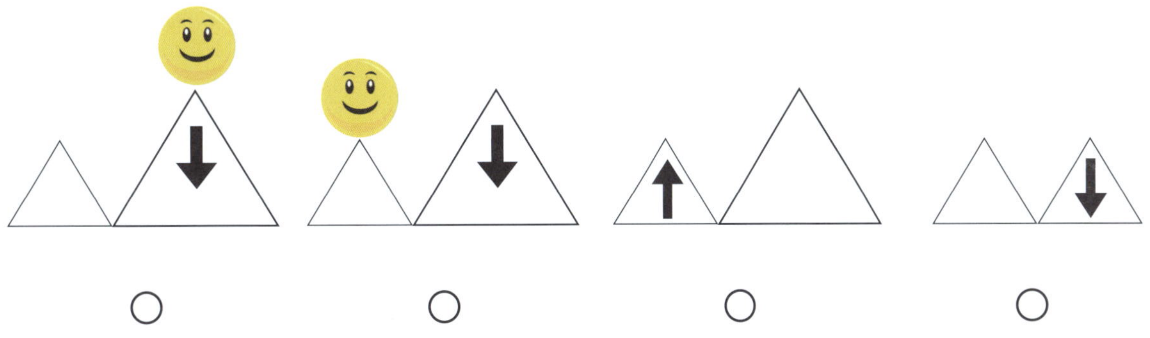

◯   ◯   ◯   ◯

© 2011 The Critical Thinking Co.™ • www.CriticalThinking.com • 800-458-4849

13.

5 6   55   5 5   56
○   ○   ○   ○

14.

5 6   55   5 5   56
●   ○   ○   ○

© 2011 The Critical Thinking Co.™ • www.CriticalThinking.com • 800-458-4849

1.

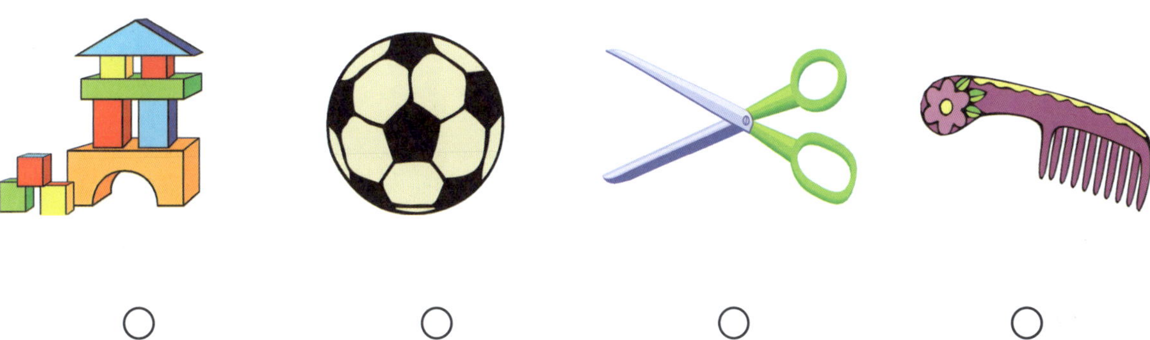

○   ○   ○   ○

2.

○   ○   ○   ○

3.

○   ○   ○   ○

4.

○   ○   ○   ○

© 2011 The Critical Thinking Co.™ • www.CriticalThinking.com • 800-458-4849

5.

6.

7.

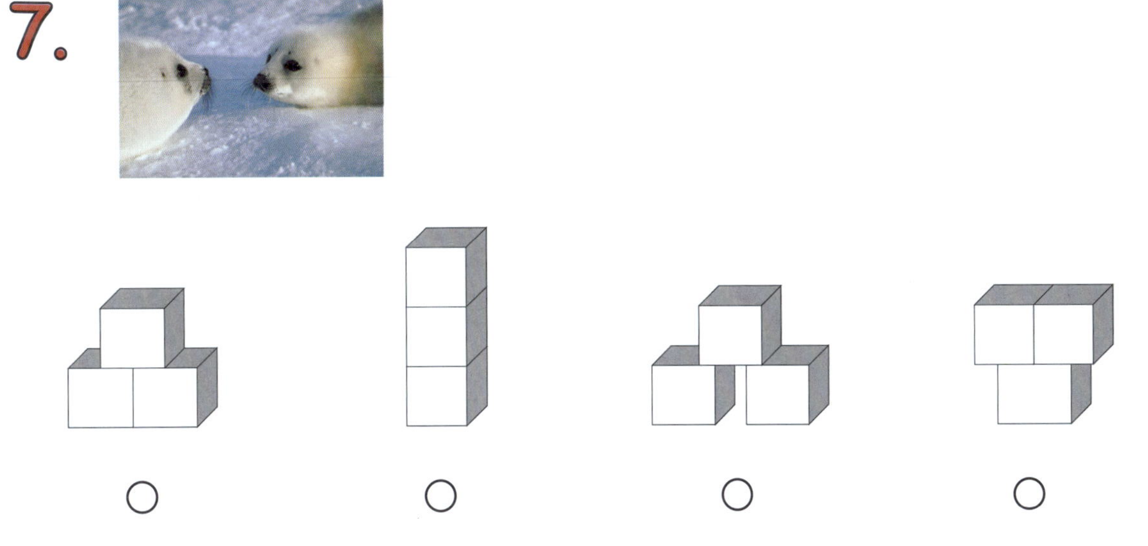

8.

○

○

○

○

9.

○

○

○

○

© 2011 The Critical Thinking Co.™ • www.CriticalThinking.com • 800-458-4849

10.

○   ○   ○   ○

11.

○   ○   ○   ○

© 2011 The Critical Thinking Co.™ • www.CriticalThinking.com • 800-458-4849

12.

  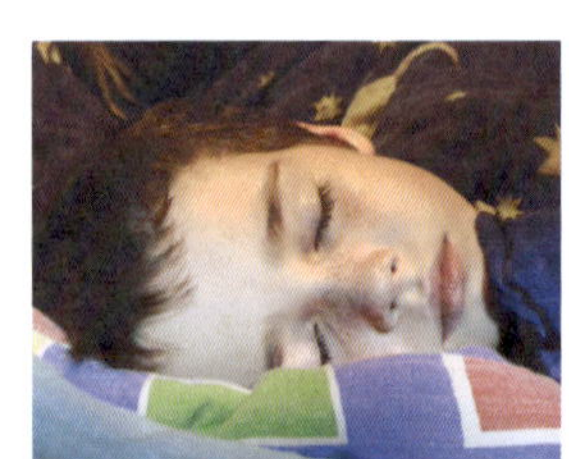 

13.

© 2011 The Critical Thinking Co.™ • www.CriticalThinking.com • 800-458-4849

14.

○   ○

○   ○

15.

○   ○   ○   ○

© 2011 The Critical Thinking Co.™ • www.CriticalThinking.com • 800-458-4849

1.

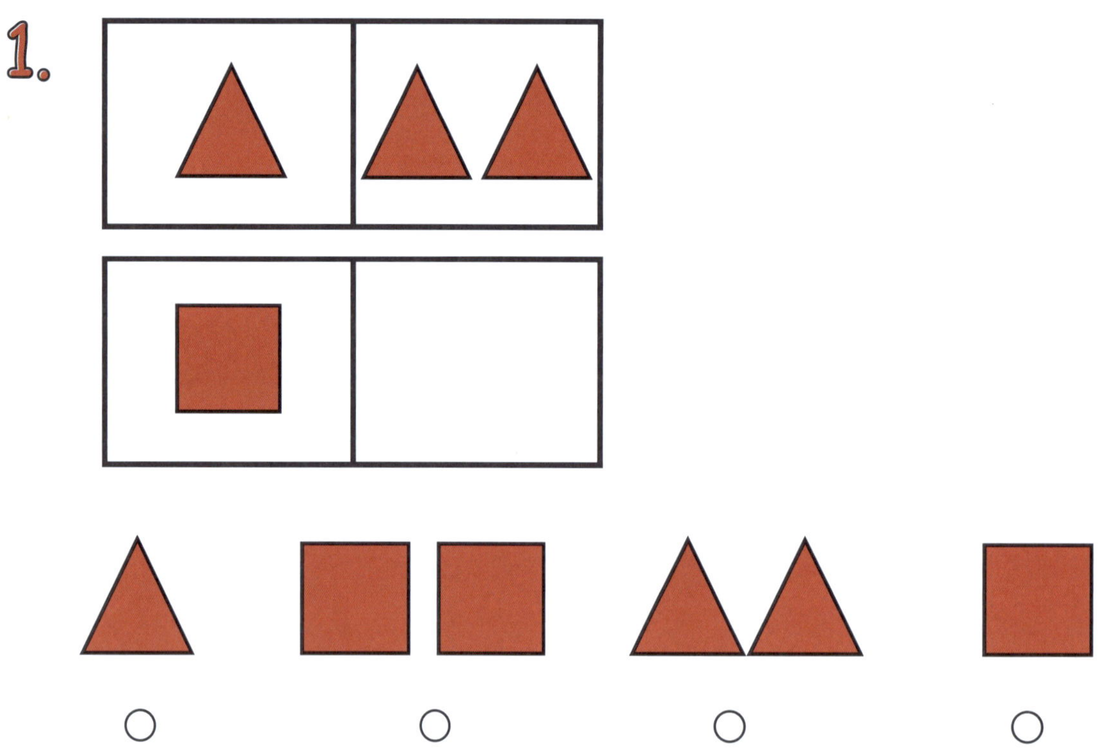

2.

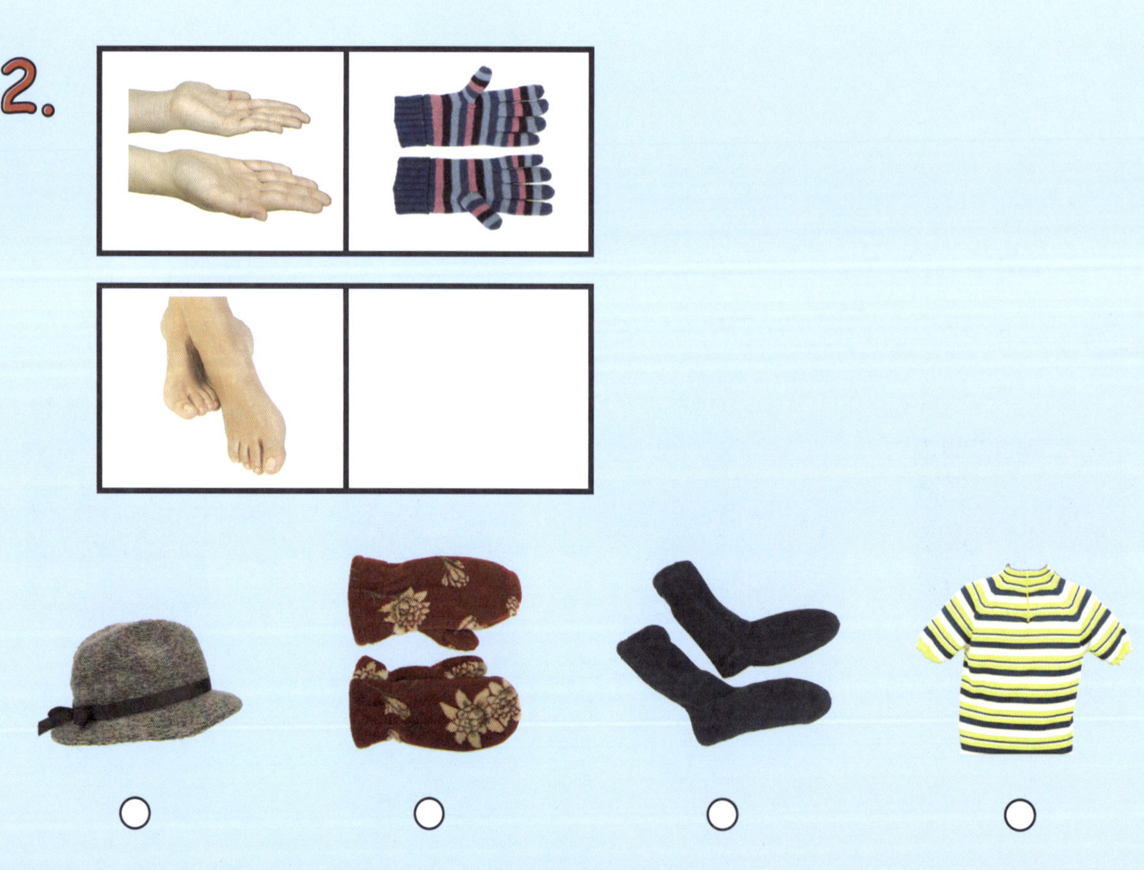

3.

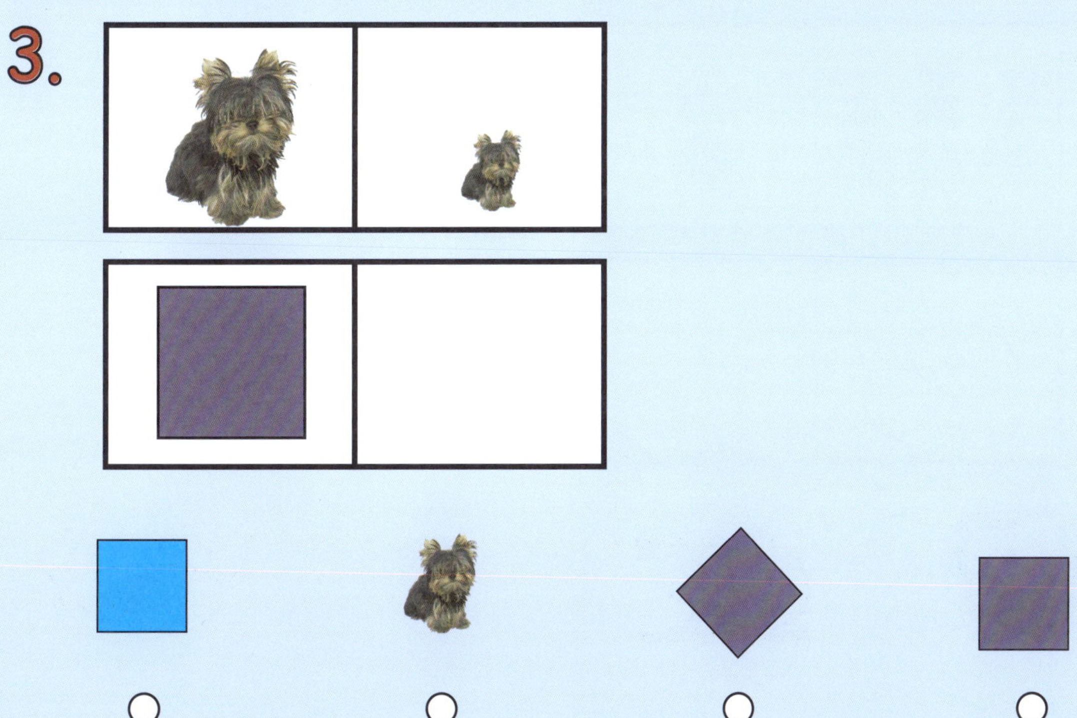

4.

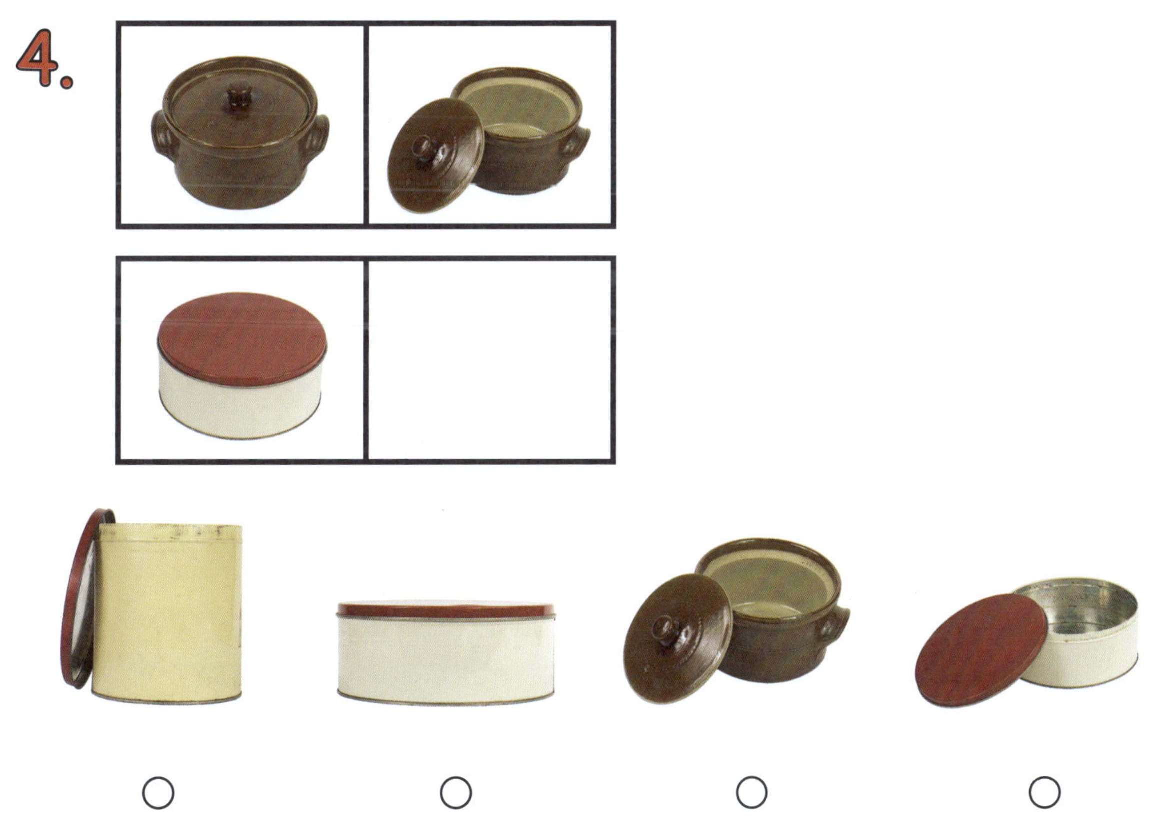

5.

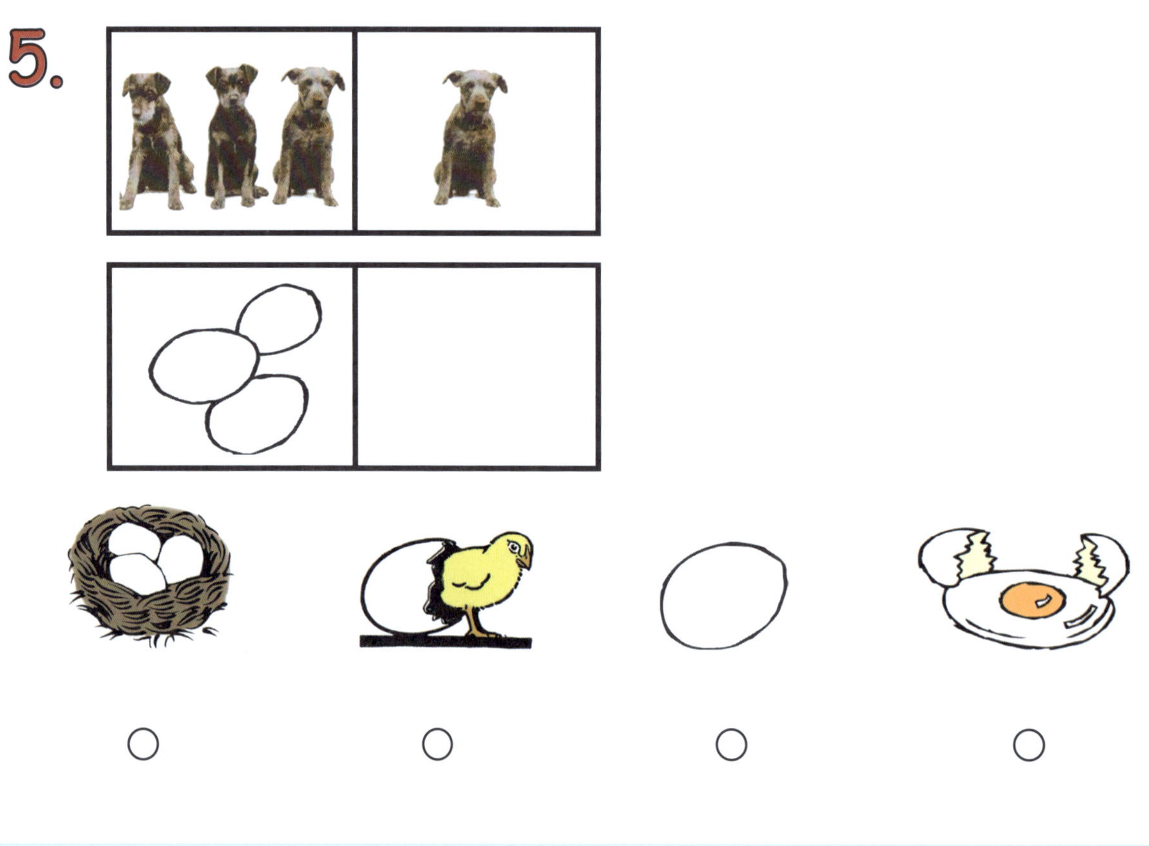

6.

© 2011 The Critical Thinking Co.™ • www.CriticalThinking.com • 800-458-4849

7.

8.

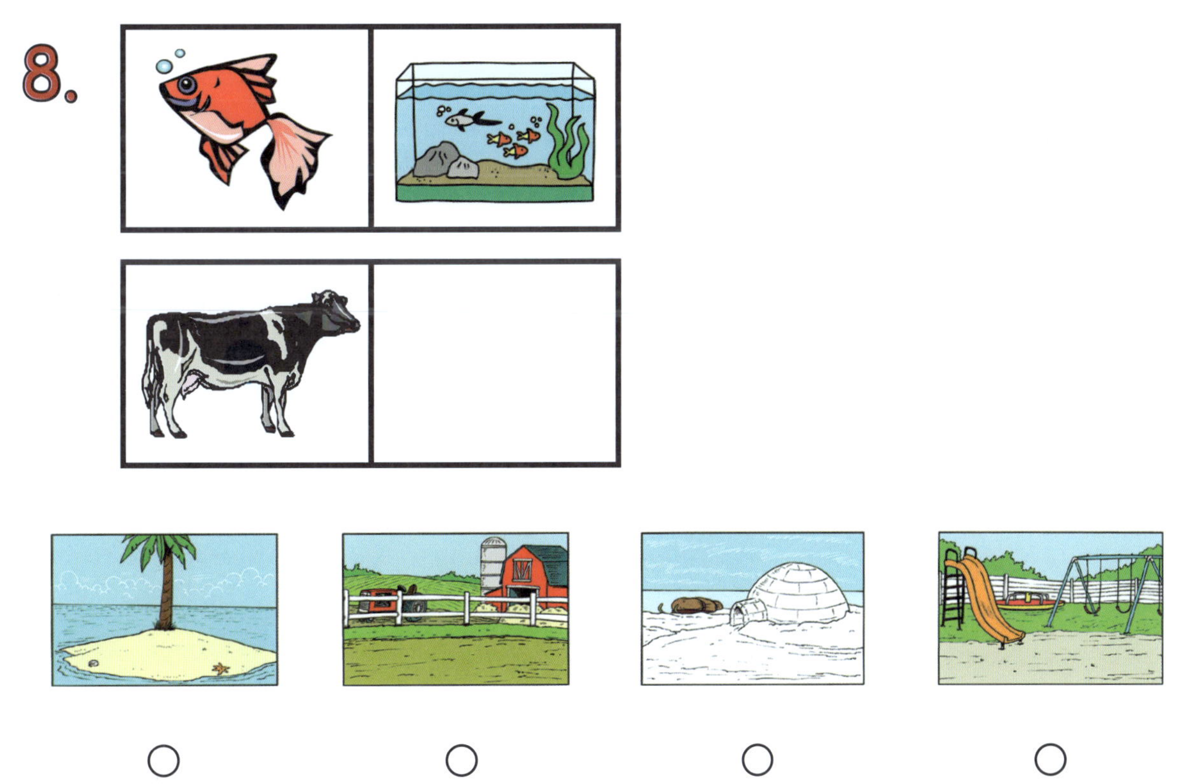

9.

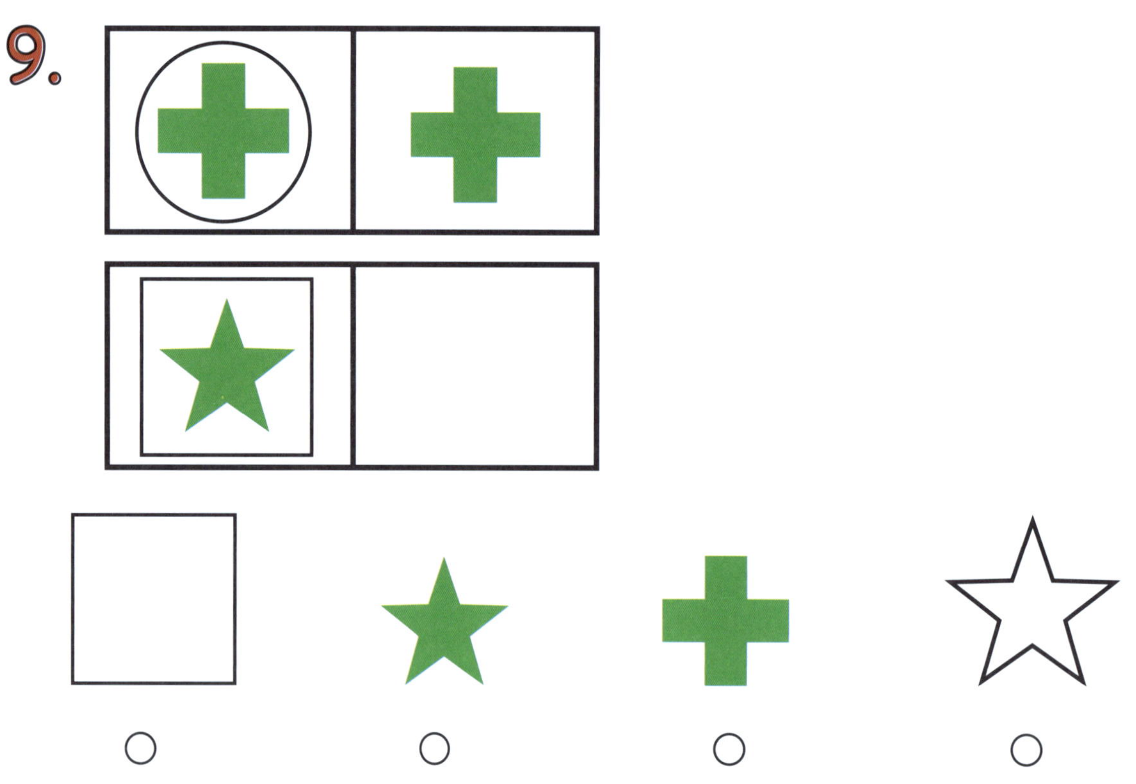

10.

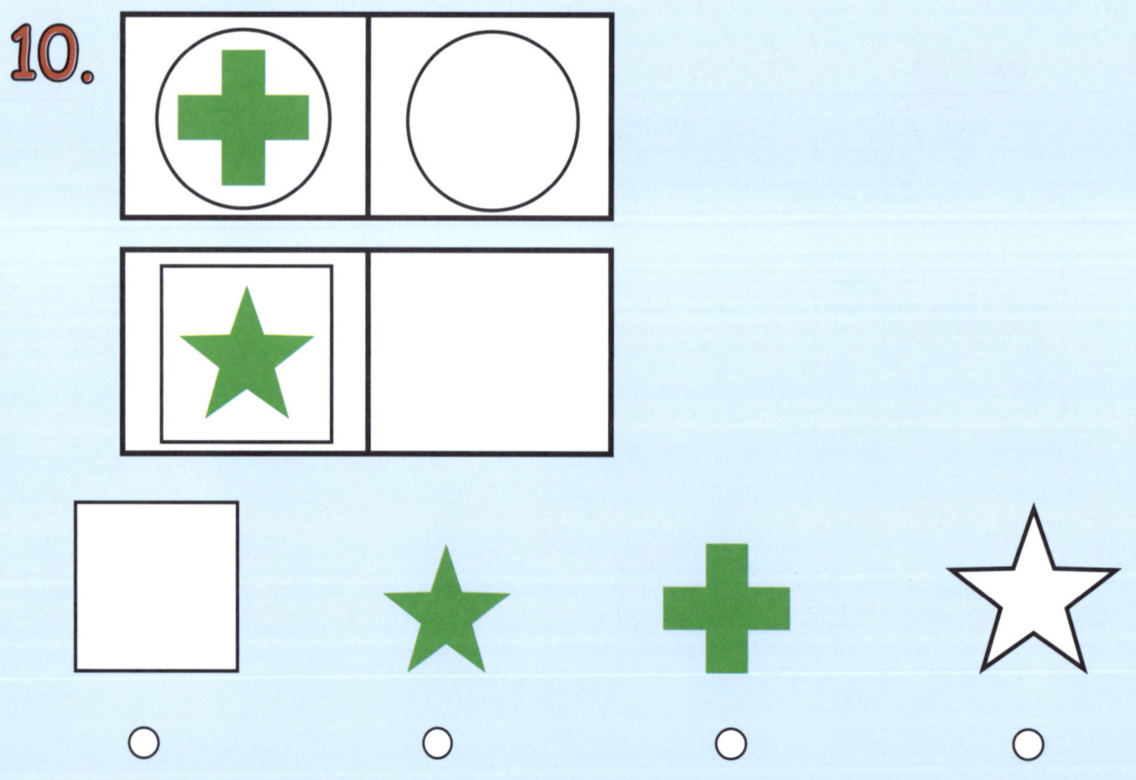

© 2011 The Critical Thinking Co.™ • www.CriticalThinking.com • 800-458-4849

11.

○   ○   ○   ○

12.

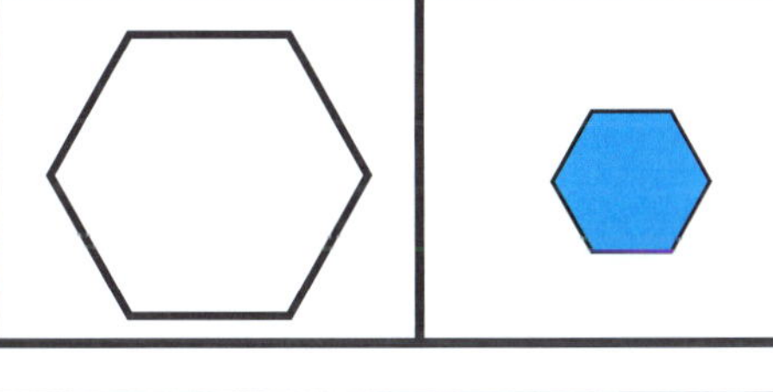

   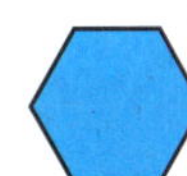   

○   ○   ○   ○

13.

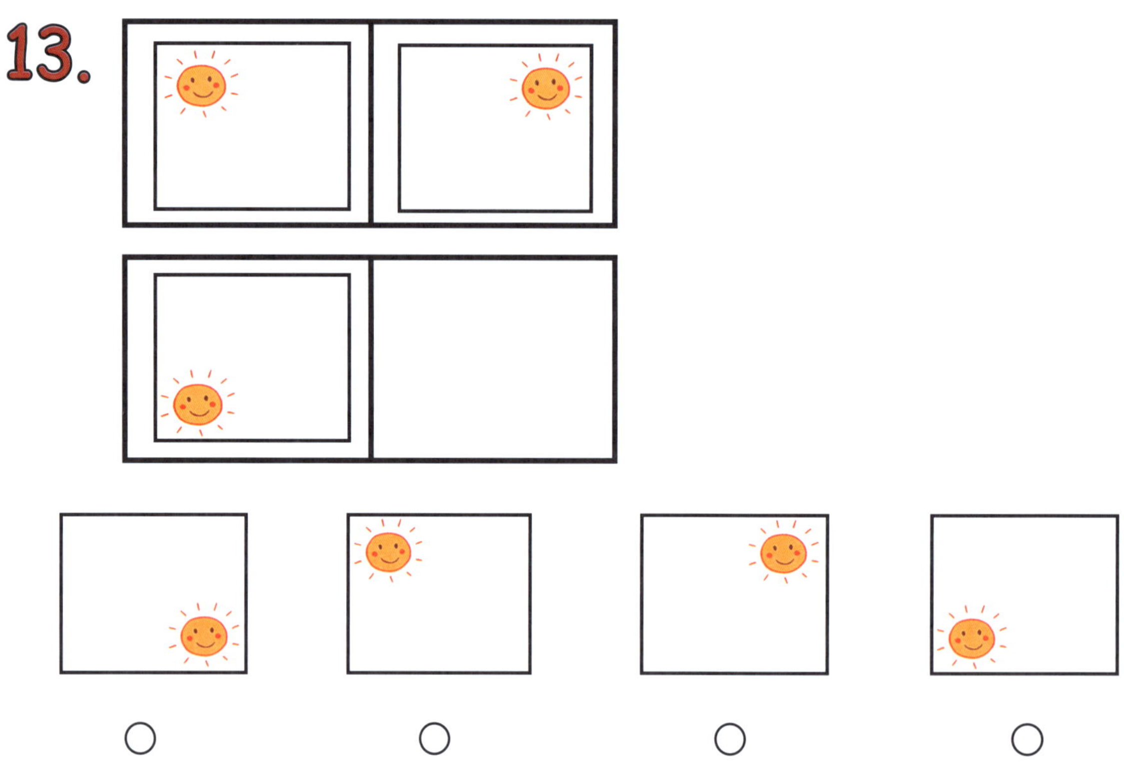

14.

© 2011 The Critical Thinking Co. ™ • www.CriticalThinking.com • 800-458-4849

1.

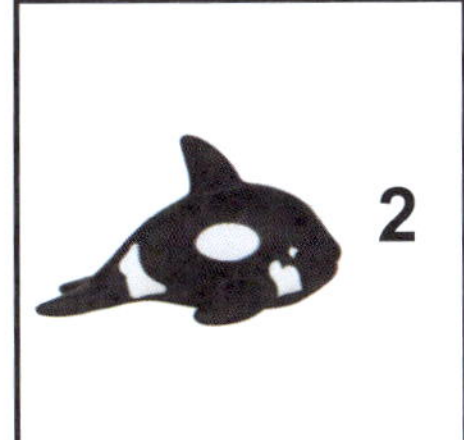 2    3    4    5

○   ○   ○   ○

2.

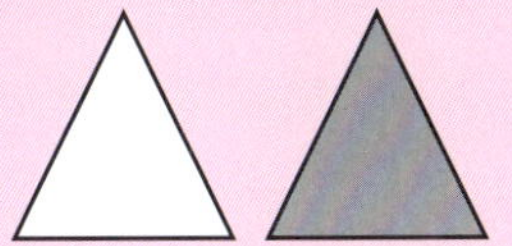      

○   ○   ○   ○

3.

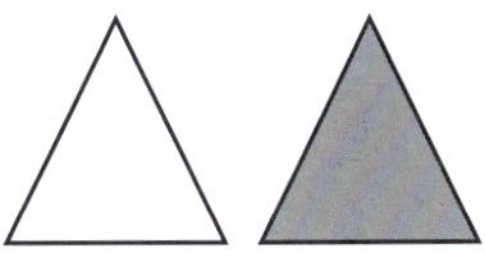   

○   ○   ○   ○

4.

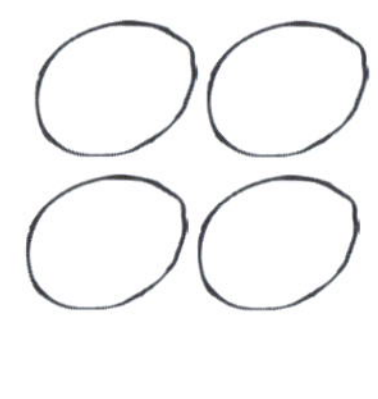
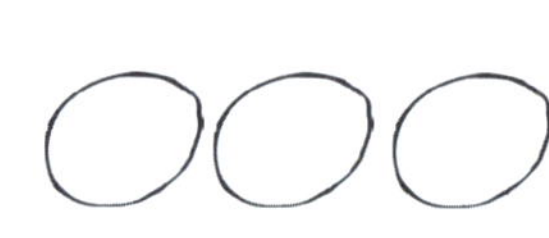
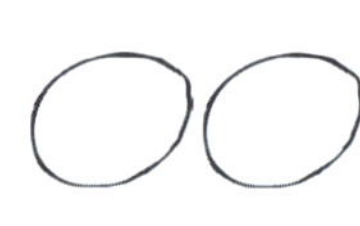

5.

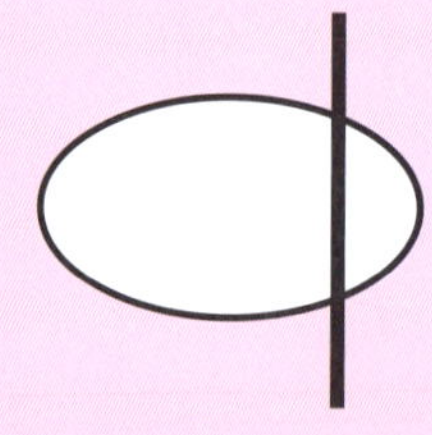
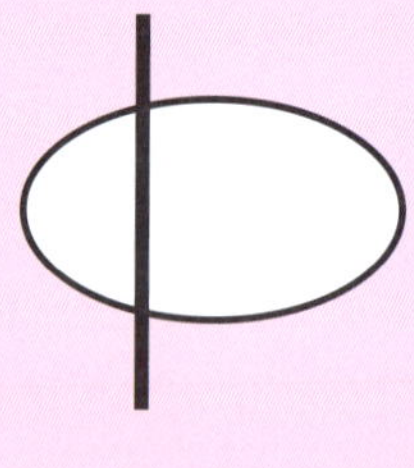

6.

© 2011 The Critical Thinking Co.™ • www.CriticalThinking.com • 800-458-4849

7.

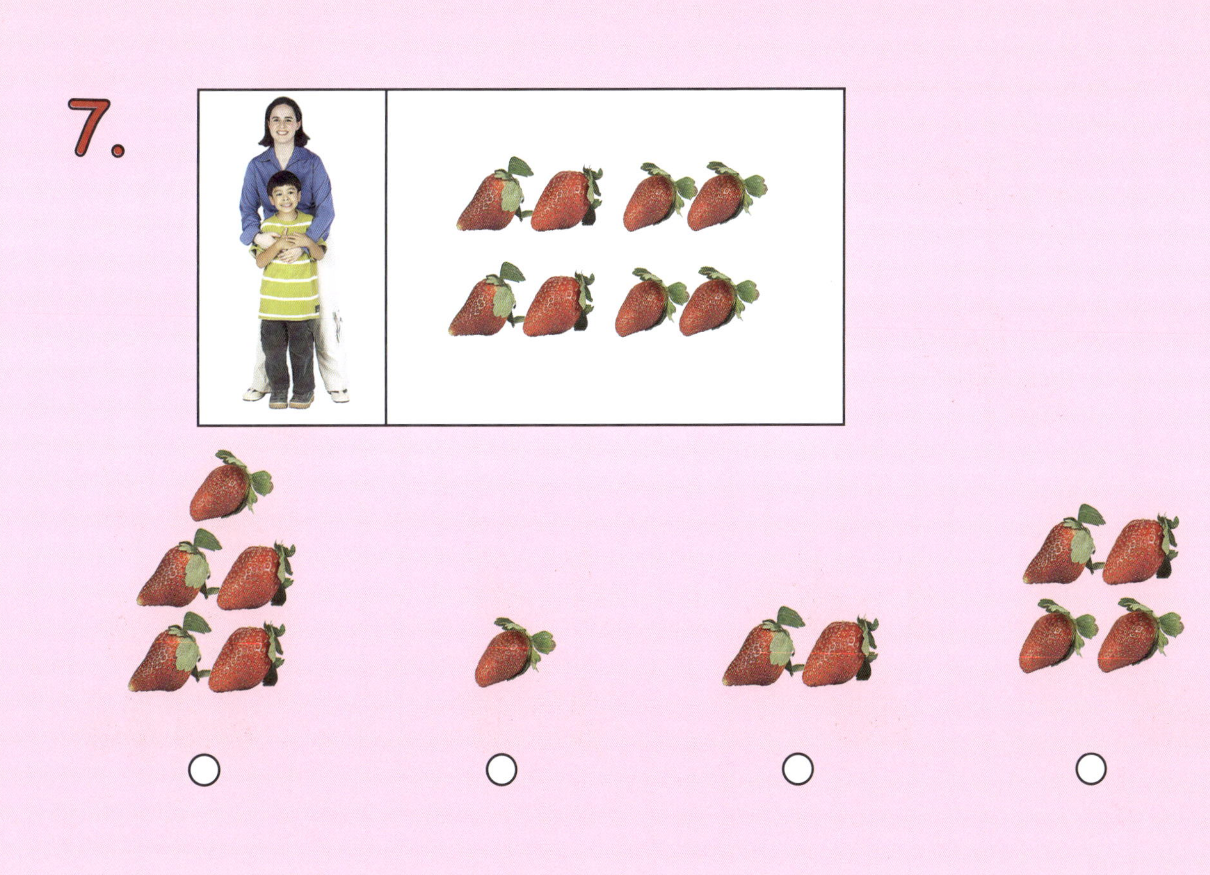

8.

© 2011 The Critical Thinking Co.™ • www.CriticalThinking.com • 800-458-4849

9.

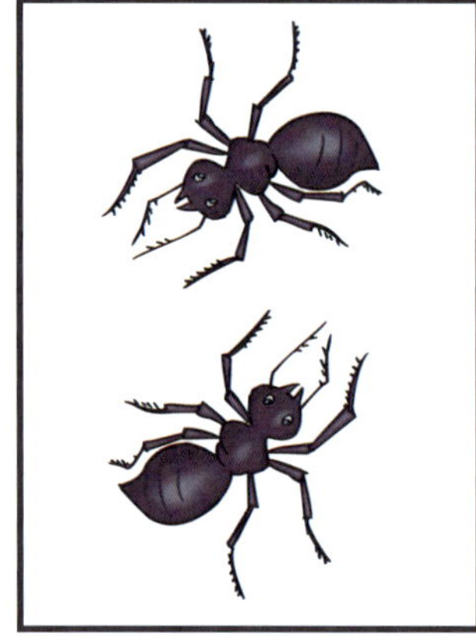

○

○

○

○

10.

○

○

○

○

© 2011 The Critical Thinking Co.™ • www.CriticalThinking.com • 800-458-4849

11.

 ○    ○    ○    ○

12.

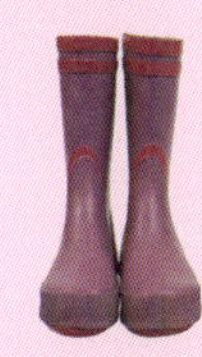 ○    ○    ○    ○

13.

 ○    ○    ○    ○

14.

15.

2   3   4   6

© 2011 The Critical Thinking Co.™ • www.CriticalThinking.com • 800-458-4849

16.

◯   ◯   ◯   ◯

17.

4   6   7   9

◯   ◯   ◯   ◯

1.

2.

© 2011 The Critical Thinking Co. ™ • www.CriticalThinking.com • 800-458-4849

3.    

○   ○   ○   ○

4.     

○   ○   ○   ○

© 2011 The Critical Thinking Co.™ • www.CriticalThinking.com • 800-458-4849

5.

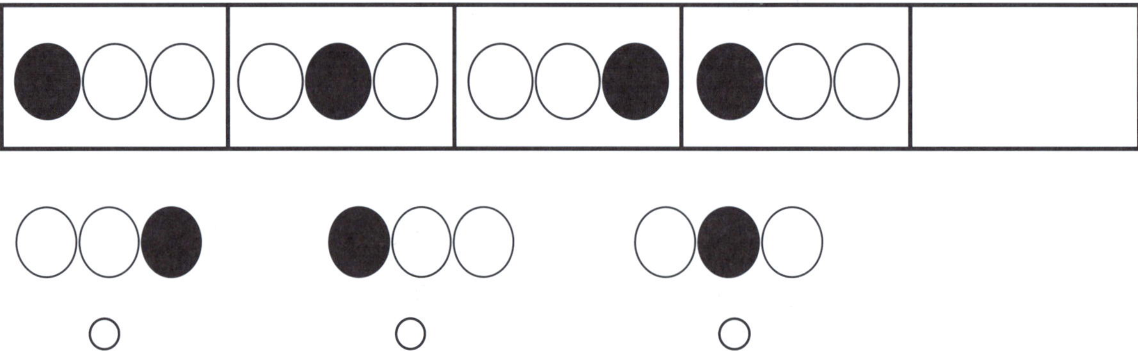

6.

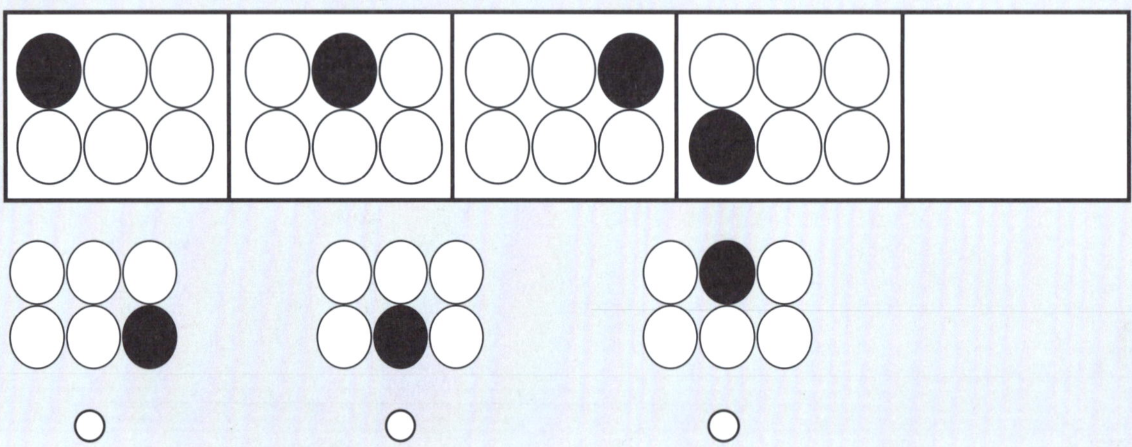

7.

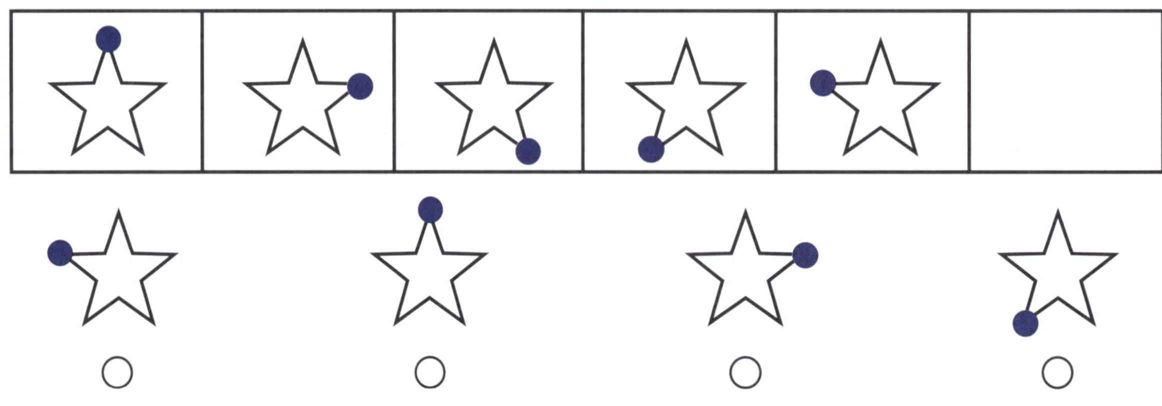

8.

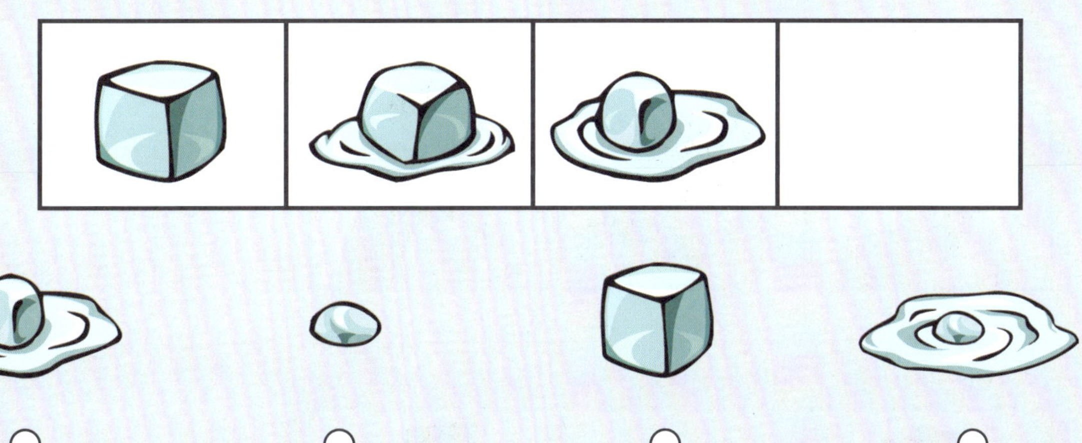

9.

10.

 ○

 ○

 ○

© 2011 The Critical Thinking Co.™ • www.CriticalThinking.com • 800-458-4849

11.

12.

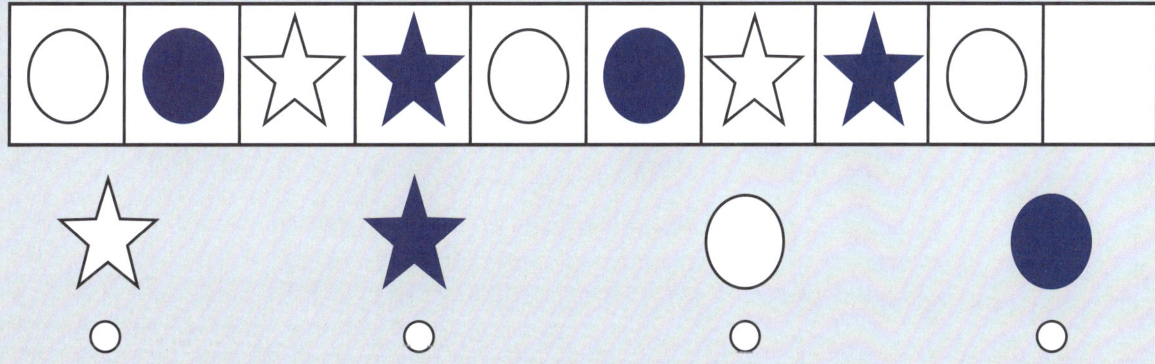

13.

14.

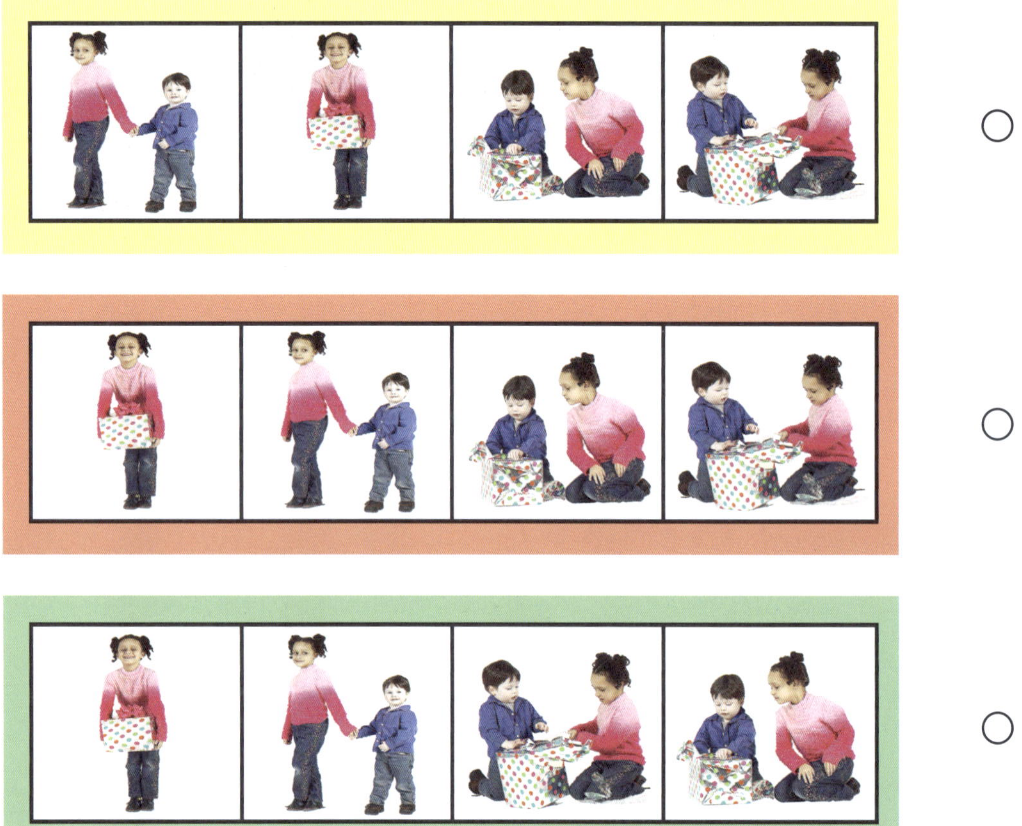

15.

© 2011 The Critical Thinking Co. ™ • www.CriticalThinking.com • 800-458-4849

1.

2.

3.

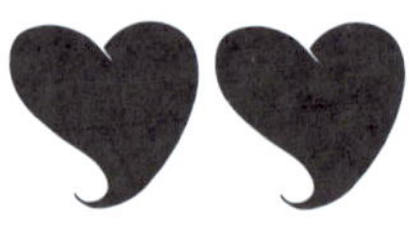

○   ○   ○   ○

4.

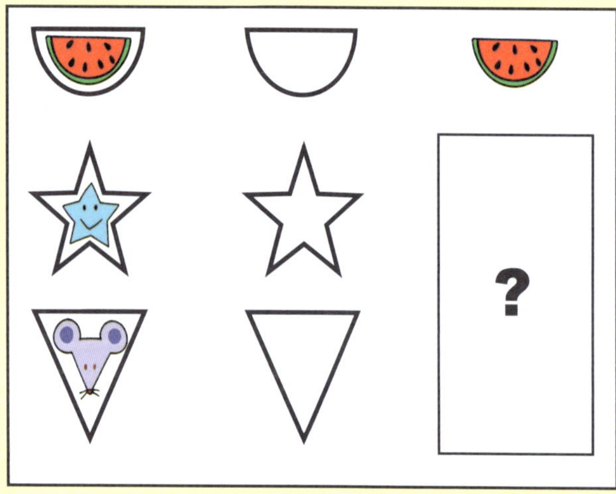

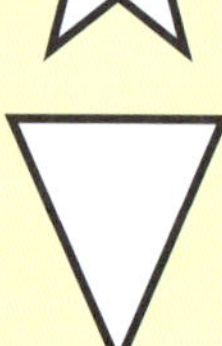

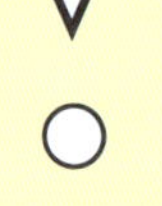

○   ○   ○   ○

© 2011 The Critical Thinking Co.™ • www.CriticalThinking.com • 800-458-4849

5.

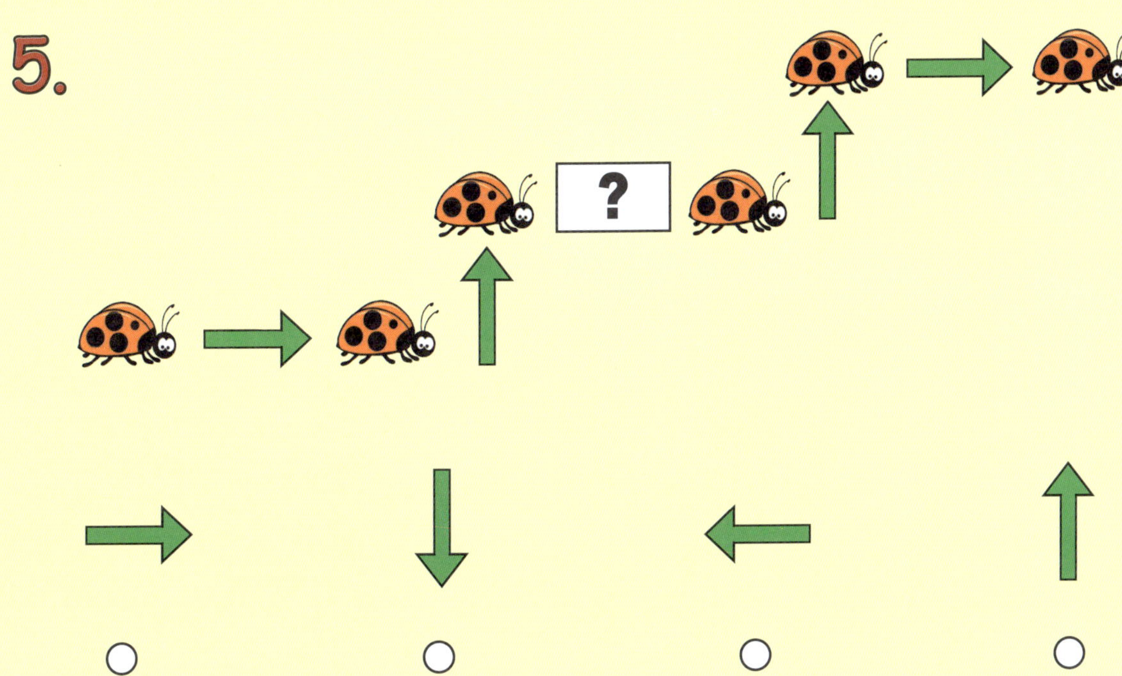

6.

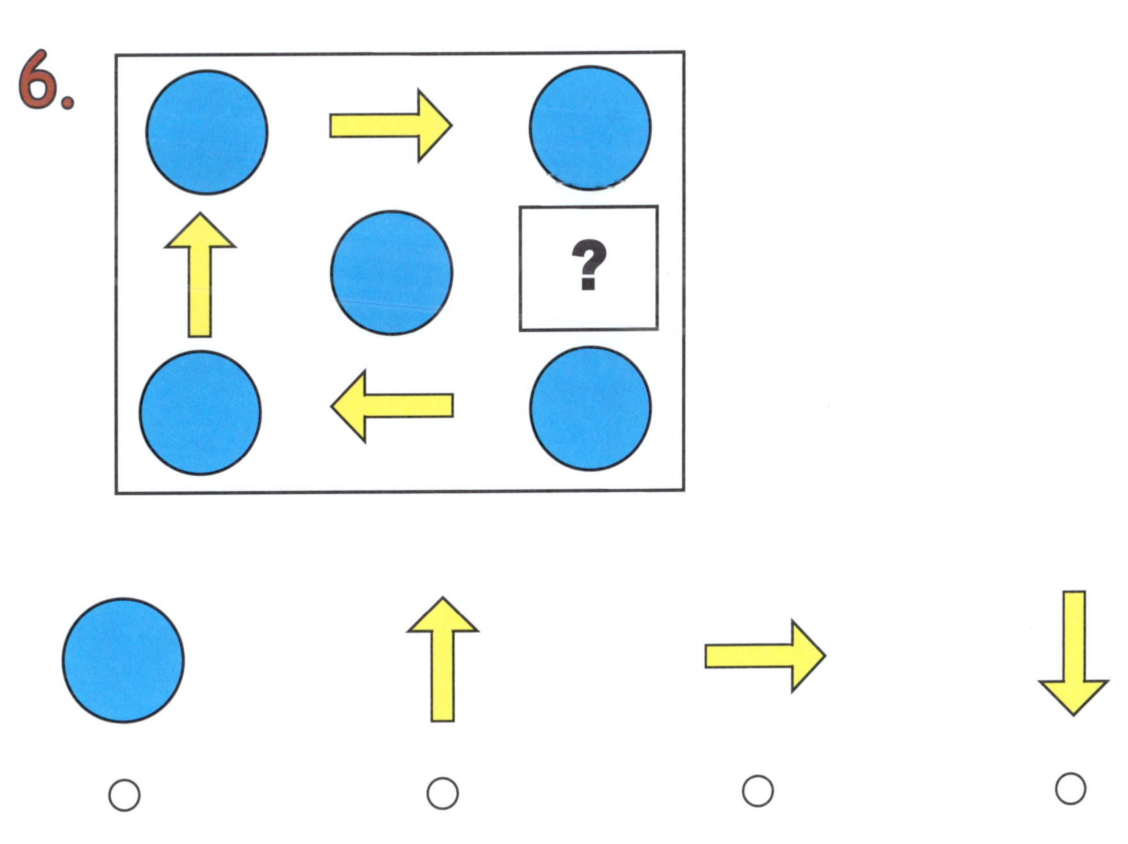

7.

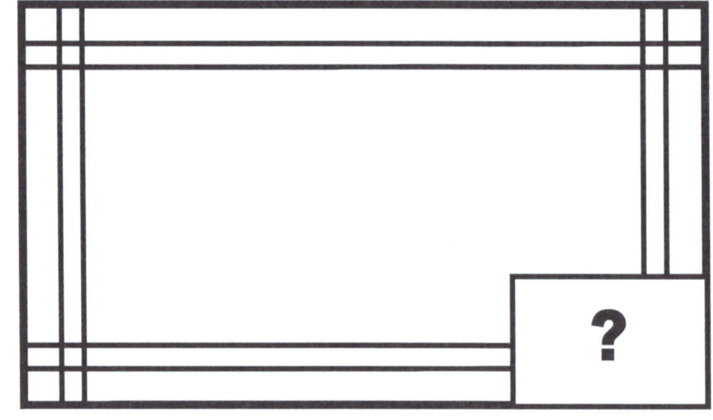

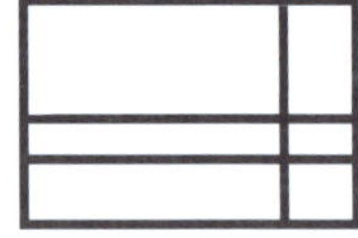  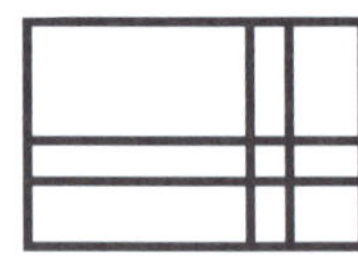 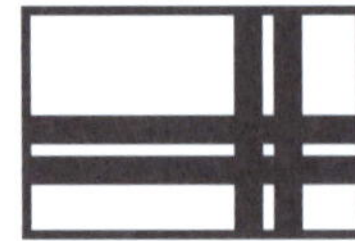

○   ○   ○   ○

8.

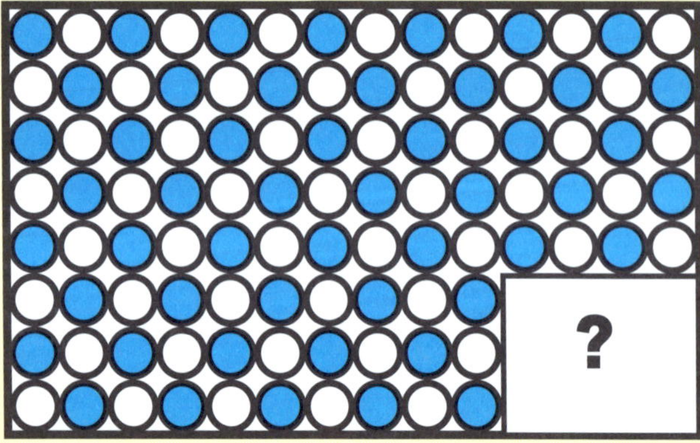

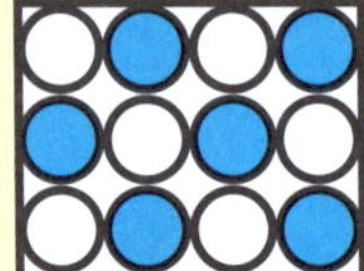 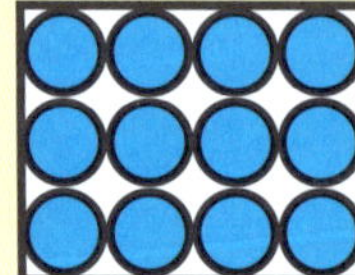 

○   ○   ○   ○

© 2011 The Critical Thinking Co.™ • www.CriticalThinking.com • 800-458-4849

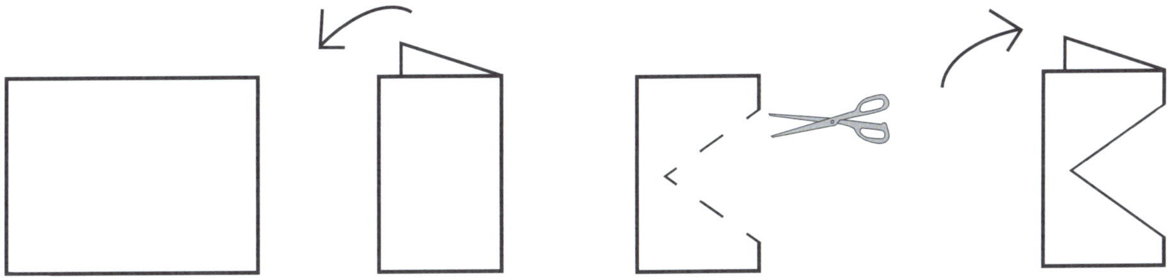

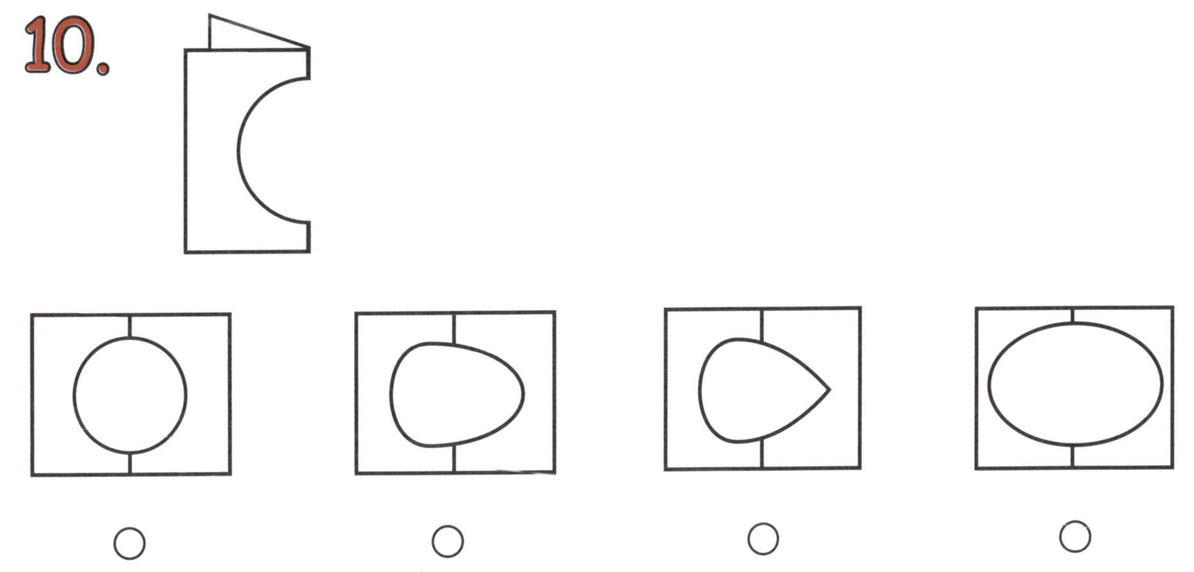

9.

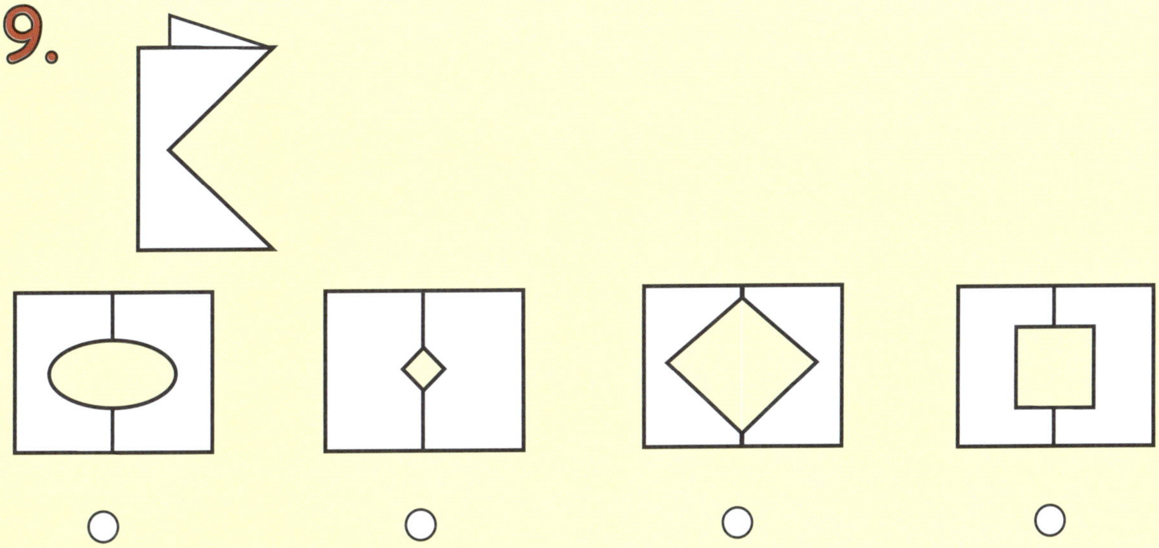

10.

11.

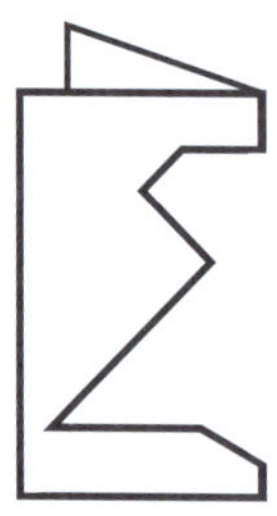

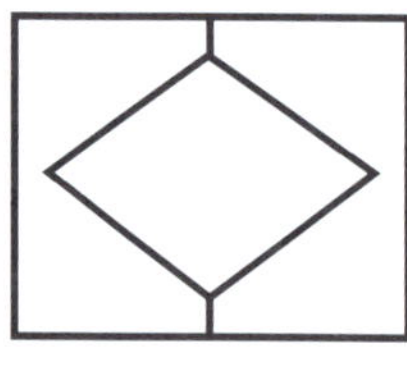         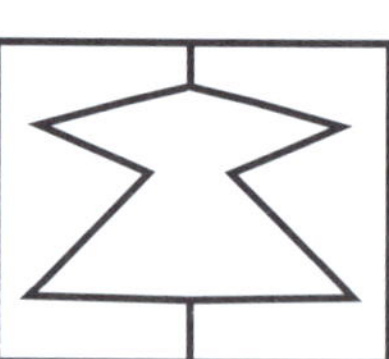

○   ○   ○   ○

12.

○   ○   ○   ○

       © 2011 The Critical Thinking Co.™ • www.CriticalThinking.com • 800-458-4849

13.

14.

○

○

○

○

© 2011 The Critical Thinking Co.™ • www.CriticalThinking.com • 800-458-4849